*To:*

_____

*From:*

_____

*Date:*

_____

The LORD bless you and keep you.

—*Numbers 6:24*

*Blessings and Promises Through the Eyes of Women of the Bible*
Copyright 2001 by Ann Spangler and Jean E. Syswerda
ISBN 0-310-98417-3

Adapted from *Women of the Bible* by Ann Spangler and Jean E.
Syswerda © 1999 by Ann Spangler and Jean E. Syswerda (Grand
Rapids, MI: Zondervan Publishing House, 1999.)

All Scripture quotations are taken from the *Holy Bible, New
International Version* (North American Edition), Copyright © 1973,
1978, 1984 by International Bible Society. Used by permission of
Zondervan Publishing House. All rights reserved.

The "NIV" and "New International Version" trademarks are
registered in the United States Patent and Trademark Office by
International Bible Society.

Requests for information should be addressed to:
    Inspirio, the gift group of Zondervan
    Grand Rapids, MI 49530
    http://www.inspiriogifts.com

Design Manager and Cover/Interior design: Amy E. Langeler
Associate Editor: Molly C. Detweiler

Printed in China

01 02 03/HK/4 3 2 1

# BLESSINGS
## and
# PROMISES
## through the EYES of
# WOMEN of the BIBLE

ANN SPANGLER &
JEAN E. SYSWERDA

inspirio

The gift group of Zondervan

# Contents

≈

Though the narratives in this book at times rely on fictional techniques to bring out various dimensions of a story and the character's emotional responses, every effort has been made to remain close to the original text, drawing out reasonable implications from Scripture's account.

Eve

*Which means*

*"life giving" or*

*"mother of all who*

*have life."*

*The LORD God caused the man to fall into a deep sleep; and while he was sleeping, he took one of the man's ribs and closed up the place with flesh. Then the LORD God made a woman from the rib he had taken out of the man, and he brought her to the man.*

*The man said,*

*"This is now bone of my bones*
*and flesh of my flesh;*
*she shall be called 'woman,'*
*for she was taken out of man." . . .*

*Now the serpent was more crafty than any of the wild animals the LORD God had made. He said to the woman, "Did God really say, 'You must not eat from any tree in the garden'?" . . .*

*When the woman saw that the fruit of the tree was good for food and pleasing to the eye, and also desirable for gaining wisdom, she took some and ate it. She also gave some to her husband, who was with her, and he ate it. Then the eyes of both of them were opened, and they realized they were naked; so they sewed fig leaves together and made coverings for themselves. . . .*

*So the LORD God said to the serpent, "Because you have done this, . . .*

*I will put enmity*
*between you and the woman,*
*and between your offspring and hers;*
*he will crush your head,*
*and you will strike his heel."*

GENESIS 2:21–23; 3:1, 6–7, 14–15

8

## Her Character

She came into the world at peace with God and Adam, the only other person on the planet. She possessed every pleasure imaginable until she listened to her enemy and began to doubt God.

---

## Her Sorrow

That she and her husband were banished from Eden and that her first son was a murderer and her second son his victim.

---

## Her Joy

That she had once tasted paradise and that God had promised her offspring would eventually destroy her enemy.

*T*he woman stirred and stretched. One finger then another moved in gentle exploration of the ground that cradled her. Her eyes opened to a Brightness, her ears to a Voice. And then a smaller voice, echoing an elated response: "This is now bone of my bones and flesh of my flesh; she shall be called 'woman,' for she was taken out of man." Adam took hold of her, and their laughter met like streams converging.

The man and the woman walked together naked and unashamed in their paradise, at ease with themselves and God. Then one day a serpent spoke to the woman: "Did God really tell you not to eat from any of the trees in the garden? God knows well that the moment you eat, your eyes will be opened and you will be like God knowing good and evil."

The woman listened. Doubt and desire pursued her until she ate the fruit and shared it with her husband. And darkness rushed on Eden.

God banished them from their garden paradise, pronouncing judgment on Eve and her husband and cursing the serpent.

Because of their sin, the curse of death fell suddenly upon the new world. So Adam and his wife fled paradise and Adam named her Eve, because she would be the mother of all the living. But her firstborn, Cain, became a murderer and her second son, Abel, his victim.

The last we see of Eve we imagine her, not as a creature springing fresh from God's hand, but as a woman in anguish. Her skin, damaged by sun and age, stretches like rough canvas across her limbs. Her hands claw the stony ground beneath her, grasping for something to ease her pain. She can feel the child inside, filling her, his body pressing to escape. The cries of mother and child meet, and Seth is born.

With her child cradled against her breast, relief spreads across Eve's face. A smile forms and then finally laughter rushes from her lips. She can't stifle her joy. For she remembers the Brightness and the Voice and the promise he gave: sooner or later, despite many griefs, her seed would crush the serpent. The woman would win.

# The Blessing of God's Grace

Embedded in the very curse put on Eve for her sin is a wonderful promise, you "*will* give birth to children" (Genesis 3:16). God's grace and mercy are marvelously evident even when he's pronouncing his judgment. When you're at your lowest, on your knees before God's judgment, never forget that his grace is still at work.

*Mercy triumphs over judgment!*

JAMES 2:13


*From the fullness of his grace we have all received one blessing after another.*

JOHN 1:16


*Where sin increased, grace increased all the more, so that, just as sin reigned in death, so also grace might reign through righteousness to bring eternal life through Jesus Christ our Lord.*

ROMANS 5:20–21


*Grace was given us in Christ Jesus before the beginning of time, but it has now been revealed through the appearing of our Savior, Christ Jesus, who has destroyed death and has brought life and immortality to light through the gospel.*

2 TIMOTHY 1:9–10

# Lot's Wife

Lot's Wife

Lot's Wi

Lot's Wife

*She is remembered*

*less for who she*

*was than for what*

*she became.*

With the coming of dawn, the angels urged Lot, saying, "Hurry! Take your wife and your two daughters who are here, or you will be swept away when the city is punished."

When he hesitated, the men grasped his hand and the hands of his wife and of his two daughters and led them safely out of the city, for the LORD was merciful to them. As soon as they had brought them out, one of them said, "Flee for your lives! Don't look back, and don't stop anywhere in the plain! Flee to the mountains or you will be swept away!" …

By the time Lot reached Zoar, the sun had risen over the land. Then the LORD rained down burning sulfur on Sodom and Gomorrah—from the LORD out of the heavens. Thus he overthrew those cities and the entire plain, including all those living in the cities—and also the vegetation in the land. But Lot's wife looked back, and she became a pillar of salt.

GENESIS 19:15–17, 23–26

## Her Character

She was a prosperous woman who may have been more attached to the good life than was good for her. Though there is no indication she participated in the sin of Sodom, her story implies that she had learned to tolerate it and that her heart had become divided as a result.

———

## Her Tragedy

That she ultimately refused God's attempts to save her.

———

*L*ot's wife had only hours to live, though she never suspected. She had married Abraham's nephew, and the two had amassed a fortune in land and livestock. Eventually, they settled in Sodom, uncomfortably comfortable in a city so wicked that heaven had dispatched angels to investigate.

Lot was at the city gate when the angels arrived. He begged them to spend the night in his home, anxious to protect them.

Just before bedtime, Lot's wife heard an ugly clamor of voices outside. A crowd of men were shouting for Lot to surrender his guests so they could abuse them as they pleased.

Finally, the angels pulled Lot back into the house and struck the men at the door blind. Then they urged Lot, "Run from this place! We are about to destroy it."

At dawn the angels again urged Lot to hurry. Still, he hesitated, until the angels grabbed Lot and the rest of his family by their hands and dragged them out, urging, "Flee for your life! Don't look back or stop anywhere on the plain!"

By the time they reached safety, the sun had risen over the land, and the city of Sodom was in flames. Men, women, children, and livestock, all were obliterated. Terrible judgment for terrible sin.

Lot and his family must have turned to each other in relief at their narrow escape and then turned again in shock, realizing that one of their number was missing. They would have searched until finally they caught sight of the white salt pillar, a lonely monument in the shape of a woman turning round toward Sodom.

Why did Lot's wife turn, despite the angel's warning? Was her heart still attached to everything she left behind in the city? Was her love of comfort and wealth a glue that caused her feet to slow, her head to turn, and her body to be overtaken by the punishment God had meant to spare her? By her own choice— her very last choice—she cast her lot with judgment rather than mercy.

Jesus urged his followers to remember Lot's wife. "Remember the wife of Lot. Whoever seeks to preserve his life will lose it, but whoever loses it will save it" (Luke 17:32–33). Sobering words recalling a sobering story, but words meant to lead us away from the compelling illusions of wickedness and safe into the arms of mercy.

# The Promise of Safety

God's angels took Lot, his wife, and his two daughters by the hand, though Lot was hesitant even to the last minute, and led them safely out of the city. God's mercy was available for Lot and his family. And his mercy is available to you as well, even in the worst of times, the most difficult situations. He's there, stretching out his hand to lead you to safety.

*The Lord is not slow in keeping his promise, as some understand slowness. He is patient with you, not wanting anyone to perish, but everyone to come to repentance.*

2 PETER 3:9

*You are my hiding place, Lord;*
*    you will protect me from trouble*
*and surround me with songs of*
*        deliverance.*

PSALM 32:7

*From the LORD comes deliverance.*
*    May your blessing be on your people.*

PSALM 3:8

*The LORD brought me out into a*
*        spacious place;*
*he rescued me because he delighted in me.*

PSALM 18:19

Rebekah

Rebekah

Rebekah

Rebekah

*Which probably*

*means "loop"*

*or "tie."*

*When I [Abraham's servant] came to the spring today, I said, "O LORD God . . . if a maiden comes out to draw water . . . and if she says to me, 'Drink, and I'll draw water for your camels too,' let her be the one the LORD has chosen for my master's son [Isaac]."*

*Before I finished praying in my heart, Rebekah came out, with her jar on her shoulder and said, . . . "Drink, and I'll water your camels too." . . . So [her brothers] sent their sister Rebekah on her way, along with her nurse and Abraham's servant and his men. . . .*

*Isaac brought [Rebekah] into the tent of his mother Sarah, and he married Rebekah. . . .*

*Isaac prayed to the Lord on behalf of his wife, because she was barren. The Lord answered his prayer, and his wife Rebekah became pregnant. . : . The Lord said to her, "Two nations are in your womb, . . . and the older will serve the younger." When the time came for her to give birth, there were twin boys in her womb. . . .*

*Rebekah said to her son Jacob, "Look, I overheard your father say to your brother Esau, 'Bring me some game and prepare me some tasty food to eat, so that I may give you my blessing in the presence of the LORD before I die.' Now, my son, listen carefully and do what I tell you: Go out to the flock and bring me two choice young goats. . . . Then take it to your father to eat, so that he may give you his blessing before he dies."*

GENESIS 24:42–46, 59, 67; 25:21,
23–24; 27:6–10

24

## Her Character

Hard-working and generous, her faith was so great that she left home forever to marry a man she had never met. Yet she played favorites with her sons, failing to trust God fully for his promises.

———

## Her Sorrow

That she was barren for the first twenty years of her married life and that she never again set eyes on her favorite son, Jacob, after he fled from his brother Esau.

———

## Her Joy

That God had gone to extraordinary lengths to pursue her, inviting her to become part of his people and his promises.

*T*urning from the well, Rebekah hoisted the brimming jug to her shoulder, welcoming its cooling touch against her skin.

As she turned to go, a stranger approached, asking for a drink. Obligingly she offered to draw water for his camels as well. She noticed the look of surprised pleasure that flashed across his face. Just moments earlier he had prayed: "If I say to a young woman, 'Please give me a little water from your jug,' and she answers, 'Drink, and I will give water to your camels, too'—let her be the one the Lord has chosen for my master's son."

A simple request. A generous response. A woman's future altered. The man Rebekah encountered at the well, Abraham's servant, had embarked on a sacred quest—to find Abraham's son Isaac a wife from among his own people.

So Isaac and Rebekah were married, and Isaac loved his wife. But it was twenty years before she gave birth—to twins. During the delivery, the youngest grasped the heel of his brother, as though striving for first position. Though second by birth, Jacob was first in Rebekah's affections. But Isaac loved Esau best.

Years later, when Isaac was old and blind, he summoned his firstborn, Esau. "Hunt some wild game for me. Prepare the kind of meal I like, and I will give you my blessing before I die."

But Rebekah devised a scheme to trick the blessing from Isaac in favor of Jacob. Disguised as Esau, Jacob presented himself to his father. So the patriarch stretched out his hand and passed the choicest blessing to his younger son.

Afraid of Esau's wrath, Rebekah persuaded Jacob to go live with her brother Laban until Esau's fury abated. But more than twenty years would pass before Jacob returned.

As a young girl, God invited Rebekah to play a vital role in the story of his people. But her heart wavered between faith and doubt, believing that God's promise required her intervention. As a result, she fostered a rivalry between her sons that separated them for most of their lives.

# The Promise of a Plan for Our Lives

Rebekah heard Abraham's servant describe how he had asked God to show him the right woman for Isaac. She knew that God had orchestrated the events himself. Still she failed to trust him to keep his promises his way. Even so, God kept his promise, using her to accomplish his plan.

God's faithfulness despite our waywardness, despite our contrariness, is evident throughout Scripture and throughout our lives. He will be faithful; he promises.

*The LORD is faithful to all his promises*
*and loving toward all he has made.*

PSALM 145:13

*Many, O LORD my God,*
*are the wonders you have done.*
*The things you planned for us*
*no one can recount to you;*
*were I to speak and tell of them,*
*they would be too many to declare.*

PSALM 40:5

*If we are faithless,*
*Jesus Christ will remain faithful,*
*for he cannot disown himself.*

2 TIMOTHY 2:13

Dear friends, do not be surprised at the painful trial you are suffering, as though something strange were happening to you. But rejoice that you participate in the sufferings of Christ, so that you may be overjoyed when his glory is revealed.

1 PETER 4:12–13

# Tamar,
## Daughter-in-law of Judah

Tamar

Tamar

Tamar

*Which means*

*"date tree" or*

*"palm tree."*

Judah got a wife for Er . . . and her name was Tamar. But Er . . . was wicked in the LORD's sight; so the LORD put him to death. Then Judah said to Onan, "Lie with your brother's wife and . . . produce offspring for your brother." But [he kept] from producing offspring . . . so [the LORD] put him to death also.

Judah then said to his daughter-in-law Tamar, "Live as a widow in your father's house until my son Shelah grows up." For he thought, "He may die too, just like his brothers." So Tamar went to live in her father's house. . . .

When Tamar was told, "Your father-in-law is on his way to Timnah to shear his sheep" she took off her widow's clothes, covered herself with a veil to disguise herself . . . for she saw that, though Shelah had now grown up, she had not been given to him as his wife.

When Judah saw her, he thought she was a prostitute. . . . Not realizing that she was his daughter-in-law, he went over to her by the roadside and said, "Come now, let me sleep with you." . . . When the time came for [Tamar] to give birth, there were twin boys in her womb.

GENESIS 38:6–11, 13–16, 27

## Her Character

Driven by one overwhelming need, she sacrificed her reputation and nearly her life to achieve her goals.

―⁓―

## Her Sorrow

That the men in her life failed to keep their promises, leaving her a childless widow.

―⁓―

## Her Joy

That her daring behavior resulted not in ruin, but in the fulfillment of her hopes to bear children.

*T*amar was the wife of Er, the eldest son of Judah, one of the founders of the twelve tribes of Israel. But Er was a wicked man, who died for his sins. In keeping with the custom of the day, Judah's second son married Tamar so that an heir could be provided for the eldest son. But he, too, behaved wickedly and died.

Already Judah had lost two sons, but he promised Tamar his youngest and only remaining son, instructing her to return to her father's house until the boy was of marriageable age. But the years passed and still there was no marriage.

One day, after Judah's wife died, he set out for Timnah to shear his sheep. Hearing the news of his journey, Tamar sat down beside the road to Timnah, disguising herself as a shrine prostitute. That day Judah slept with her, leaving behind his personal seal, cord and staff in pledge of future payment.

About three months later, Judah learned of Tamar's pregnancy. Outraged, he ordered her burned to death. But Tamar sent him a stunning message: "It is by the man to whom these things belong that I am with child."

The man who so quickly passed judgment, little heeding his own tryst with a prostitute, was suddenly taken up short. To his credit, he said, "She is more righteous than I am, since I did not give her to my son."

Tamar gave birth to twins. As with Jacob and Esau, the children struggled in her womb. A tiny hand came out and then disappeared, but not before being tied with a scarlet thread by the midwife. Then a small, slippery body emerged, but with no trace of the red thread. They named the first boy Perez (meaning, "breach"). Then the little one with the ribbon around his wrist was born and they named him Zerah, (meaning "scarlet"). Perez was recognized as the first-born.

Distasteful as the story is, God used Tamar's determination to ensure that the tribe of Judah would not only survive but would one day bear the world's Messiah. From Judah's line would come King David and finally, hundreds of years later, Jesus Christ.

## The Promise of a Plan for Our Good

The story in Genesis 38 reveals nothing about Tamar's knowledge of God's hand in the events of her life. More than likely, she was unaware of the power of God at work. But he was there nevertheless, bringing good out of evil and blessing out of less than honorable events.

That's the beauty of this story. God's power to bring positive things from the negative, even sinful, events of our lives is just as much at work now as in Tamar's day. We may not see it today or tomorrow—or perhaps ever—but we can trust the God we love to fulfill the plans he has made.

*Not one of all the good promises the LORD your God gave you has failed. Every promise has been fulfilled; not one has failed.*

JOSHUA 23:14


*We know that in all things God works for the good of those who love him, who have been called according to his purpose.*

ROMANS 8:28


*You intended to harm me, but God intended it for good.*

GENESIS 50:20

Jochebed

*Which means*

*"the Lord*

*is glory."*

*Pharaoh gave this order to all his people: "Every [Hebrew] boy that is born you must throw into the Nile." . . .*

*Now a man of the house of Levi married a Levite woman [Jochebed], and she became pregnant and gave birth to a son. When she saw that he was a fine child, she hid him for three months. But when she could hide him no longer, she got a papyrus basket . . . [and] placed the child in it and put it among the reeds along the bank of the Nile. His sister stood at a distance to see what would happen to him.*

*Then Pharaoh's daughter went down to the Nile to bathe. . . . She saw the basket among the reeds . . . and saw the baby. He was crying, and she felt sorry for him. "This is one of the Hebrew babies," she said.*

*Then his sister asked Pharaoh's daughter, "Shall I go and get one of the Hebrew women to nurse the baby for you?"*

*"Yes, go," she answered. And the girl went and got the baby's mother. . . . So the woman took the baby and nursed him.*

EXODUS 1:22; 2:1–9

## Her Character

Her fierce love for her son, coupled with her faith, enabled her to act heroically in the midst of great oppression.

---

## Her Sorrow

To live in bondage as a slave.

---

## Her Joy

That God not only preserved the son she surrendered to him, but that he also restored her child to her.

She held the baby to her breast, muffling his cries with her sobs. Though a slave in Egypt, Jochebed was yet a Levite, a woman who belonged to the God of Abraham and Sarah, the God who had promised that his people would one day be as numerous as the sand of the sea. Now they were so numerous that the Pharaohs worried the Israelites might one day betray the nation from within. So Pharaoh commanded his soldiers to throw every newborn Hebrew male into the waters of the Nile. Jochebed could hear the screams as children were torn from their mothers' arms.

Her own arms tightened around her baby. This one, she vowed, would never be fed to the Egyptian river god.

For three months, as long as she dared, she hid the infant. Finally, she acted on an idea. Pharaoh had commanded that her son be thrown into the Nile River. All right then. Her own hands would consign him to the water.

Jochebed bent down and laid her son in a papyrus basket. Then, with a whispered prayer , she wiped the tears from her eyes and begged God to preserve her baby from the crocodiles that swarmed the river.

Unable to bear the pain of watching her baby drift away from her, she instructed her daughter Miriam to keep the child in sight from her vantage point on the banks of the river.

Soon Pharaoh's daughter arrived at the riverbank. Spotting the basket among the reeds, she sent her slave girl to fetch it. As soon as she saw the little one, she loved him. The river had brought her a child whom she would cherish as her own.

Was she surprised when a young slave girl, Miriam, asked whether she could fetch a Hebrew woman to nurse the baby for her? Did she suspect the truth when Jochebed gathered the boy in her arms, this time as his nursemaid?

Whatever was in her mind, she named the child Moses, saying "I drew him out of the water." For the next forty years, she educated him, a prince in the courts of Pharaoh himself.

Two women—a slave and a princess—preserved the life of Israel's future deliverer and so preserved the entire Israelite race.

# The Promise of Freedom

Jochebed had one thing in mind when leaving Moses in a basket in the river—to preserve his life for one more day, one more hour, one more moment. She could not have realized God was putting into place a divine plan to rescue his people from the oppression they were suffering.

God's ways are beautiful in the extreme. He uses the fierce love of a mother to bring freedom to an entire race. Jochebed's story can help us realize that God is always to be trusted.

*Moses [said to the Israelites], "Do not be afraid. Stand firm and you will see the deliverance the LORD will bring you today. The Egyptians you see today you will never see again. The LORD will fight for you; you need only to be still."*

EXODUS 14:13–14

*The plans of the LORD stand firm forever, the purposes of his heart through all generations.*

PSALM 33:11

*I run in the path of your commands, LORD, for you have set my heart free.*

PSALM 119:32

*If the Son sets you free, you will be free indeed.*

JOHN 8:36

# Rahab

Rahab

Rahab

Rahab

*Which means*

*"storm,"*

*"arrogance,"*

*"broad," or*

*"spacious."*

*Then Joshua son of Nun secretly sent two spies from Shittim. "Go, look over the land," he said, "especially Jericho." So they went and entered the house of a prostitute named Rahab and stayed there. . . .*

*Before the spies lay down for the night, she went up on the roof and said to them, "I know that the LORD has given this land to you and that a great fear of you has fallen on us, so that all who live in this country are melting in fear because of you. . . . Now then, please swear to me by the LORD that you will show kindness to my family, because I have shown kindness to you. . . .*

*Then [the Israelites] burned the whole city and everything in it, but they put the silver and gold and the articles of bronze and iron into the treasury of the LORD's house. But Joshua spared Rahab the prostitute, with her family and all who belonged to her, because she hid the men Joshua had sent as spies to Jericho—and she lives among the Israelites to this day.*

JOSHUA 2:1, 8–9, 12; 6:24–25

## Her Character

Rahab was wise as well as clever. She saw judgment coming and was able to devise an escape plan for herself and her family. As soon as she heard what God had done for the Israelites, she cast her lot with his people, risking her life in an act of faith.

---

## Her Sorrow

To see her own people destroyed and her city demolished.

---

## Her Joy

That God had given her, a prostitute and a foreigner, the opportunity to know him and belong to his people.

As well as entertaining locals, Rahab welcomed guests from various caravans whose routes crisscrossed Jericho. Men from all over the East brought news of a swarm of people, encamped east of the Jordan River. Rahab heard marvelous stories about the exploits of their God, how he had dried up the Red Sea so they could escape their Egyptian slave masters, and how he had trained and toughened the Israelites for forty years in the desert. Such news spread fear throughout Jericho.

When two Israelite spies made their way to Rahab's house, she hid them. Later, when she received a message from the king of Jericho inquiring about the spies, Rahab lied in order to save them: "The men you speak of came to me, but at dark they left, and I do not know where they went. You will have to pursue them immediately to overtake them."

As soon as the king's men left, she warned her guests: "I know that the LORD has given you the land. . . . Now then, swear to me by the Lord that, since I am showing kindness to you, you in turn will show kindness to my family . . . and save us from death."

Quickly, the two men handed her a scarlet cord, instructing Rahab to tie it in the window. Their people, they promised, would see it and spare everyone inside. With that they slipped out the window and scrambled down the city walls.

Later, Rahab watched from her window as the Israelites gathered around the city. Her eyes followed the curious scene: seven priests were carrying an ark, followed by thousands of men, marching around the city walls. The spectacle repeated itself for the next five days. Then, as the sun rose on the seventh day, she watched as they marched several times around Jericho. As they completed their seventh turn, Rahab heard the ram's horn and a thunderous cry of voices. Suddenly the city walls collapsed. The invading army killed everyone inside, sparing only Rahab and her family.

A prostitute and foreigner, she is the only woman singled out by name and commended for her faith in Hebrews 11. Her own people destroyed, Rahab left everything behind, eventually becoming an ancestor of King David and, therefore, one of Jesus' ancestors as well.

# The Blessing of God's Use of Ordinary People

The story of Rahab reveals again God's willingness to use the less than perfect, the outcast, the unsuitable, to accomplish his purposes. God doesn't wait for us to become perfect or totally mature in our faith in order to use us. He only asks that we be willing, as Rahab was. He does not promise to make us perfect and *then* to use us, but, like Rahab, he promises to use us and *through* that experience to perfect us.

*For Christ's sake, I delight in weaknesses, in insults, in hardships, in persecutions, in difficulties. For when I am weak, then I am strong.*

2 CORINTHIANS 12:10

*When the kindness and love of God our Savior appeared, he saved us, not because of righteous things we had done, but because of his mercy.*

TITUS 3:4–5

*I saw the Lord seated on a throne, high and exalted, and the train of his robe filled the temple. . . .*

*"Woe to me!" I cried. "I am ruined! For I am a man of unclean lips, and I live among a people of unclean lips, and my eyes have seen the King, the LORD Almighty." Then one of the seraphs flew to me with a live coal in his hand, which he had taken with tongs from the altar. With it he touched my mouth and said, "See, this has touched your lips; your guilt is taken away and your sin atoned for."*

*Then I heard the voice of the Lord saying, "Whom shall I send? And who will go for us?"*

*And I said, "Here am I. Send me!"*

ISAIAH 6:1, 5–8

Jael

*Which means*

*"a wild or*

*mountain*

*goat."*

Then Deborah said to Barak, "Go! This is the day the LORD has given Sisera into your hands. . . ." So Barak went down Mount Tabor, followed by ten thousand men. At Barak's advance, the LORD routed Sisera and all his chariots and army. . . . All the troops of Sisera fell by the sword; not a man was left.

Sisera, however, fled on foot to the tent of Jael. . . . Jael went out to meet Sisera and said to him, "Come, my lord, come right in. Don't be afraid." So he entered her tent, and she put a covering over him. "I'm thirsty," he said. "Please give me some water." She opened a skin of milk, gave him a drink, and covered him up. . . .

Jael, Heber's wife, picked up a tent peg and a hammer and went quietly to him while he lay fast asleep, exhausted. She drove the peg through his temple into the ground, and he died.

JUDGES 4:14–19, 21

## Her Character

Decisive and courageous, she seized the opportunity to slay an enemy of God's people.

---

## Her Joy

To be lauded by the prophetess Deborah and the Jewish leader Barak for her part in a decisive victory.

*J*ael watched uneasily through the flaps of her tent as clouds swept the blue from the sky and heavy rain fell. Sisera, she knew, had marched to Tabor. But what good were iron chariots in a flooded valley, she wondered? The Israelites were poorly armed with little chance of prevailing. Still, she remembered the stories of Moses and the victories their God had given the Israelites.

The sight of a man running, then stumbling toward her interrupted her thoughts. A soldier fleeing? Was he Israelite or Canaanite? His identity might reveal the way the winds of battle were blowing. She went out to meet him, surprised to find that Sisera himself was approaching.

"Come in, my lord, come in with me; do not be afraid," she welcomed him.

"Please give me a little water to drink. I am thirsty," he said. So she gave him a drink and then covered him.

"Stand at the entrance of the tent," he said to her. "If anyone comes and asks, 'Is there someone here?' say, 'No!'"

As soon as Sisera fell into an exhausted sleep, Jael picked up a tent peg and hammer. Her arm was steady, her aim sure. Hadn't she been in charge of setting up the tents all these years? Quickly, she thrust the peg through his temple and into the ground. Like a piece of canvas fixed in place, Sisera, the great general, lay dead, slain by a woman's hand, just as Deborah had prophesied to Barak.

Was Jael a hero, an opportunist, or merely a treacherous woman? It is difficult to know. Perhaps she believed in Israel's God. Perhaps she merely wanted to curry favor with the day's clear winners. Certainly Barak and Deborah approved of her, singing:

"Blessed among women be Jael,
Blessed among tent-dwelling women."

The story strikes us as bloodthirsty, all the more so because we don't usually attribute such behavior to a woman. But by the standards of ancient warfare, Jael was a hero. Decisive and courageous, she was a woman who helped God's people at a critical moment in history.

# The Promise to Save Us from Our Enemies

Behind the gruesome story of Jael is a God who promises never to forget his people. When hope seems dim and the prospect of victory seems nearly impossible, God is at work, saving his people from their enemies.

The people of Israel must have worn God to exasperation. When times were good they easily forgot God and went their own way. But as soon as times got tough, they went running to him for deliverance.

Sound like anyone you know? We too think we can handle it all, until we run up against something too hard for us. Only then do we run to God for help.

God wants us to make him our refuge at all times, not just when we are desperate. If we rely on him daily, it will be impossible to forget his many kindnesses.

*God has rescued us from the dominion of darkness and brought us into the kingdom of the Son he loves, in whom we have redemption, the forgiveness of sins.*

COLOSSIANS 1:13–14

*When [your people] cried out to you again, you heard from heaven, LORD, and in your compassion you delivered them time after time.*

NEHEMIAH 9:28

*I love you, O LORD, my strength . . .*
*    I call to the LORD, who is worthy*
*        of praise,*
*and I am saved from my enemies.*

PSALM 18:1, 3

*The Lord will rescue me from every evil attack and will bring me safely to his heavenly kingdom.*

2 TIMOTHY 4:18

Delilah

*Which means*

*"dainty one."*

*[Samson] fell in love with . . . Delilah. The rulers of the Philistines went to her and said, "See if you can lure him into showing you the secret of his great strength . . . so we may . . . subdue him. Each one of us will give you eleven hundred shekels of silver."*

*So Delilah said to Samson, "Tell me the secret of your great strength." . . . Samson answered her, "If anyone ties me with seven fresh thongs that have not been dried, I'll become as weak as any other man." . . . [So] she tied him with them. . . . But he snapped the thongs as easily as a piece of string snaps when it comes close to a flame. So the secret of his strength was not discovered. . . .*

*[After Samson had lied to her three times] she said to him, "How can you say, 'I love you,' when you won't confide in me?" . . .*

*So he told her everything. "No razor has ever been used on my head," he said, "because I have been a Nazirite set apart to God since birth. If my head were shaved, my strength would leave me, and I would become as weak as any other man."*

*When Delilah saw that he had told her everything, she sent word to the rulers of the Philistines, "Come back once more; he has told me everything." . . . Having put him to sleep on her lap, she called a man to shave off the seven braids of his hair, and so began to subdue him. And his strength left him.*

JUDGES 16:4–9, 15–19

## Her Character

Delilah used her beauty to betray her lover and enrich herself.

---

## Her Sorrow

That Samson lied to her, making her look foolish on three different occasions.

*H*er teeth gleamed white in the dusky light; a smile parted lips soft and smooth as a scarlet ribbon. Fortune had come knocking on her door that day. Delilah was sure that no other lover had ever paid her so well as Samson would.

The Philistine kings hated the long-haired strongman from Israel, and each had offered her an incredible sum for betraying him. She had merely to deliver the secret of his strength.

But Samson kept tricking her with crazy stories every time she asked him about the source of his strength. Finally Delilah confronted him, "How can you say you love me when you won't confide in me?" Worn down by her nagging, Samson gave in. "No razor has touched my head," he confided. "If my head were shaved, my strength will leave me!"

Before birth, Samson had been consecrated to God. An angel had appeared to his mother instructing her never to cut his hair.

Sensing she had heard the truth at last, Delilah had Samson's hair cut while he slept one day. The Philistines quickly took him captive, gouging out his eyes and imprisoning him.

That's the last we hear of the lovely, treacherous, and now wealthy Delilah, but not the last we hear of her lover. One day the Philistines held a great celebration in honor of Dagon, god of the harvest. They brought Samson out of prison, gloating over their once-mighty enemy. But when Samson stood among the pillars of their temple, he prayed for one more surge of strength. Then he braced himself against the two central pillars of the temple and pushed. The roof collapsed, and Samson and his enemies were buried together under its rubble.

The strange story of Samson and Delilah is hardly edifying. It's tempting to conclude that the selfish, ill-disciplined Samson had finally met his match in the greedy Delilah. If anything, this sordid tale assures us that God will use anything and anyone to accomplish his purposes, even our sin, even our enemies. Our deliverance is purely a matter of grace. But how much better if we become people whose inner strengths match our outer strengths, enabling us to live out the role God intends, assured of his pleasure.

# The Blessing of God's Forgiveness

Even the sordid story of Delilah and her Hebrew lover Samson conveys an important truth: God loves us and will not abandon us even when we make mistakes, even when we sin. But forgiveness is hardly an excuse to keep on sinning. Though God used Samson to destroy the enemies of his people, Samson perished along with his Philistine captors. We must always remember that although God is forgiving, he is also just. He will forgive, but he will also allow us to reap the consequences of our sin. But we can take heart that even terrible consequences can be a part of God's plan to perfect us.

*Remember not the sins of my youth*
  *and my rebellious ways;*
*according to your love remember me,*
  *for you are good, O LORD.*

PSALM 25:7


*The LORD upholds all those who fall*
  *and lifts up all who are bowed down.*

PSALM 145:14


*"I will forgive their wickedness and will*
*remember their sins no more," says the Lord.*

HEBREWS 8:12

# Naomi

Naomi

Naomi

Naomi

*Which means*

*"my joy" or*

*"pleasant."*

Elimelech, Naomi's husband, died, and she was left with her two sons. They married Moabite women, one named Orpah and the other Ruth. After they had lived there about ten years, both Mahlon and Kilion also died. . . . "Don't call me Naomi," she told [the people of Bethlehem]. "Call me Mara, because the Almighty has made my life very bitter. I went away full, but the LORD has brought me back empty. . . . So Naomi returned from Moab accompanied by Ruth the Moabitess, her daughter-in-law, arriving in Bethlehem. . . .

Boaz announced to the elders and all the people, "Today you are witnesses that I have bought from Naomi all the property of Elimelech, Kilion and Mahlon. I have also acquired Ruth the Moabitess, Mahlon's widow, as my wife, in order to maintain the name of the dead with his property, so that his name will not disappear from among his family or from the town records." . . .

So Boaz took Ruth and she became his wife. Then . . . she gave birth to a son. The women said to Naomi: "Praise be to the LORD, who this day has not left you without a kinsman-redeemer. May he become famous throughout Israel! He will renew your life and sustain you in your old age. For your daughter-in-law, who loves you and who is better to you than seven sons, has given him birth."

Then Naomi took [Ruth's] child, laid him in her lap and cared for him.

RUTH 1:3–5, 20–22; 4:9–10, 13–16

## Her Character

Suffering a three-fold tragedy, Naomi refused to hide her sorrow or bitterness. Believing in God's sovereignty, she attributed her suffering to his will. But her fixation on circumstances, both past and present, led to hopelessness. A kind and loving mother-in-law, she inspired unusual love and loyalty in her daughters-in-law.

---

## Her Sorrow

To have lost a husband and two sons in a foreign land, far from family and friends.

---

## Her Joy

To have returned safely to Bethlehem with her daughter-in-law Ruth, who would eventually rekindle her happiness and hope.

*T*hough Naomi could see for miles from her vantage point high on the road that led from Moab to Judah, she could glimpse nothing at all of her future. Instead, her thoughts were fixed on the past.

Ten years ago, she and Elimelech had lived happily in Bethlehem. But the city whose name meant "house of bread" suddenly had none, so they migrated to the highlands of Moab to escape the famine. Though her husband died, her two sons settled down and married Moabite women. But then both of them died.

Now Naomi had only her widowed daughters-in-law, Ruth and Orpah, to keep her company. Together they had cried and comforted each other, finally deciding to leave Moab for Bethlehem. But once on the road, Naomi decided it wasn't right for the young women to forsake their families and friends for so uncertain a future.

"Go back, each of you, to your mother's house!" she told them. "May the Lord be kind to you as you were to the departed and to me! May the Lord grant each of you a husband and a home in which you will find rest."

The three women embraced, tears streaking their cheeks. Then Orpah kissed her mother-in-law good-bye and left. But Ruth clutched Naomi and whispered fiercely, "Wherever you go I will go, and wherever you lodge I will lodge, your people shall be my people, and your God my God. Wherever you die I will die, and there be buried."

The old woman's stubbornness was no match for the younger woman's love. And so Naomi and Ruth continued on to Bethlehem. After so long an absence, Naomi's return created a great commotion in the town, and all the women welcomed her, saying, "Can this be Naomi?"

"Don't call me Naomi," she told them. "Call me Mara [meaning 'bitter'], for the Almighty has made it very bitter for me. I went away with an abundance, but the Lord has brought me back destitute."

Naomi's grief made it difficult for her to see beyond her circumstances. Had she known the blessings yet in store, she might not have felt so bitter. Though she couldn't know it, she was beginning a new episode in her life's story, a story that was full of hope.

# The Promise of a Future Filled with Hope

God's faithfulness to restore to fullness an empty life is revealed more in this story of Naomi than in any other biblical account. She had lost everything, but through the love and obedience of Ruth and Boaz, Naomi became a grandmother, and an ancestor of the Messiah.

Like Naomi, we may have trouble recognizing God's goodness and his faithfulness at times. But he is still with us no matter the circumstances. Even when our days are darkest, we can rest in God's promise of a future filled with hope.

*You will restore my life again, O LORD.*

PSALM 71:20

*"I will repay you for the years the locusts*
      *have eaten. . . .*
*You will have plenty to eat, until you*
      *are full,*
      *and you will praise the name of the*
      *LORD your God,*
      *who has worked wonders for you,"*
      *says the LORD.*

JOEL 2:25–26

   *"For I know the plans I have for you,"*
*declares the LORD, "plans to prosper you*
*and not to harm you, plans to give you hope*
*and a future."*

JEREMIAH 29:11

# Ruth

Ruth

Ruth

Ruth

*Which means*

*"friendship."*

Ruth . . . said to Naomi, "Let me go to the fields and pick up the leftover grain behind anyone in whose eyes I find favor." . . . So she went out and began to glean in the fields behind the harvesters. As it turned out, she found herself working in a field belonging to Boaz, who was from the clan of Elimelech. . . .

So Boaz said to Ruth, "My daughter, listen to me. Don't go and glean in another field and don't go away from here. Stay here with my servant girls. . . . Whenever you are thirsty, go and get a drink from the water jars the men have filled."

At this, she bowed down with her face to the ground. She exclaimed, "Why have I found such favor in your eyes that you notice me—a foreigner?"

Boaz replied, "I've been told all about what you have done for your mother-in-law since the death of your husband. . . . May the LORD repay you for what you have done. May you be richly rewarded by the LORD, the God of Israel, under whose wings you have come to take refuge." . . .

Then Boaz announced to the elders and all the people, "Today you are witnesses that. . . . I have . . . acquired Ruth the Moabitess, Mahlon's widow, as my wife" . . .

So Boaz took Ruth and she became his wife. . . . The LORD enabled her to conceive, and she gave birth to a son.

RUTH 2:2–3, 8–12; 4:9–10, 13

## Her Character

Generous, loyal, and loving, she is strong and serene, able to take unusual risks, dealing actively with the consequences.

———

## Her Sorrow

To have lost her husband, homeland, and family.

———

## Her Joy

To discover firsthand the generous, loyal, and loving nature of God, as he provided her with a husband, a son, and a home to call her own.

*I*t was harvest time in Israel when Boaz first laid eyes on the young woman toiling in his field. According to Israel's law, the poor had the right to gather whatever the harvesters missed. And Ruth was certainly poor, a Moabite widow who had traveled with Naomi to Bethlehem. He couldn't help noticing how efficiently she worked, quickly stuffing the grain into a coarse sack, resting only for a moment. He knew how dangerous gleaning could be for an attractive young foreigner, so he instructed the men working the fields to be kind to her.

Everyone in Bethlehem had been talking about Ruth and about Naomi's unexpected return. He had heard of their shared tragedy and Ruth's extraordinary loyalty toward his relative Naomi. A man could wish for such a friend as Ruth had been to Naomi.

One evening Boaz and his men lay down under the stars near the harvested grain. In the middle of the night he woke with a start, realizing a woman was lying at his feet. "I am your servant, Ruth," she whispered. "Spread the corner of your cloak over me, for you are my next of kin."

He could hardly believe her words. The young woman had risked her reputation by lying down with him. Quickly he covered her, saying, "May the Lord bless you, my daughter! I will do for you whatever you say." Soon after, Boaz and Ruth were married, and God blessed them with a son, whom they named Obed.

Shortly after his son's birth, Boaz watched as Naomi held her grandson to her breast. Surrounded by the other women of Bethlehem, she closed her eyes, listening to the women's prayer regarding the child: "Blessed is the Lord who has not failed to provide you today with an heir! May he become famous in Israel! He will be your comfort and the support of your old age, for his mother is worth more to you than seven sons!"

Yes, Boaz thought, his Ruth was better than seven sons. But even he couldn't have realized how greatly God had blessed him in the person of Ruth. For their son Obed became the father of Jesse and Jesse the father of David. In addition to being King David's great-grandparents, both Boaz and Ruth are mentioned in the genealogy of Jesus, who would become the Savior of the world.

# The Blessing of a Generous Heart

Ruth made a promise on the road to Bethlehem that she was determined to keep. She had no way of knowing that her way of blessing Naomi would eventually become a blessing in her own life. That's the divine irony of our God, who delights so much in seeing us love and bless others that he turns that love and blessing back on us in double measure.

*A generous man will prosper;*
  *he who refreshes others will himself*
    *be refreshed.*

PROVERBS 11:25

*Blessed are the merciful,*
  *for they will be shown mercy.*
*Blessed are the pure in heart,*
  *for they will see God.*

MATTHEW 5:7–8

*Jesus said, "Behold, I am coming soon!*
*My reward is with me, and I will give to*
*everyone according to what he has done."*

REVELATION 22:12

*Serve wholeheartedly, as if you were*
*serving the Lord, not men, because you*
*know that the Lord will reward everyone for*
*whatever good he does.*

EPHESIANS 6:7–8

# Tamar,
## Daughter of
## King David

Tamar

Tamar

Tamar

*Her brother*

*took advantage*

*of her*

*innocence.*

Amnon son of David fell in love with Tamar, the beautiful sister of Absalom son of David. Amnon became frustrated to the point of illness on account of his sister Tamar, for she was a virgin, and it seemed impossible for him to do anything to her. . . .

So Amnon lay down and pretended to be ill. When the king came to see him, Amnon said to him, "I would like my sister Tamar to come and make some special bread in my sight." . . . So Tamar . . . made the bread in his sight and baked it. . . . But when she took it to him to eat, he grabbed her and said, "Come to bed with me, my sister."

"Don't, my brother!" she said to him. "Don't force me. Such a thing should not be done in Israel! Don't do this wicked thing." . . .

But he refused to listen to her, and since he was stronger than she, he raped her.

Then Amnon hated her with intense hatred, . . . Amnon said to her, "Get up and get out!" . . .

So his servant put her out and bolted the door after her. . . . Tamar put ashes on her head and tore the ornamented robe she was wearing. She put her hand on her head and went away, weeping aloud as she went. Her brother Absalom said to her, "Has that Amnon, your brother, been with you? Be quiet now, my sister; he is your brother. Don't take this thing to heart." And Tamar lived in her brother Absalom's house, a desolate woman.

2 SAMUEL 13:1–2, 6, 8, 11–12, 14–15, 18–20

## Her Character

Tamar shared her father David's good looks. Young and innocent, she was naïve to the danger that threatened from her own family circle.

—–∿–—

## Her Sorrow

That her half brother saw her only as an object for his lust, destroying her future as a result, and that her father the king did nothing to protect her.

*K*ing David's daughter, Tamar, probably lived a protected life, perhaps destined for a marriage that would strengthen the king's political alliances. But all the precautions in the world couldn't save her from the danger that threatened from David's inner circle.

Amnon was David's heir. As the king's eldest son, he was used to getting his way. But lately he had grown despondent. Something was gnawing at his heart, chasing away his sleep.

One day Jonadab, Amnon's cousin, asked him: "Why are you so dejected?"

Amnon confided in his friend, saying, "I am in love with Tamar, my brother Absalom's sister."

"Lie down on your bed and pretend to be sick," Jonadab shrewdly advised. "When your father comes to visit you, say to him, 'Please let my sister Tamar come and encourage me to take food.'"

So David, concerned for his son, sent his daughter into a trap that would ruin her life. As soon as Tamar entered Amnon's bedroom, he grabbed hold of her. Though Tamar begged him to let her go, Amnon forced himself on his half-sister.

As soon as the storm of his passion died, his infatuation turned to hatred. He threw Tamar out of his house, as though she, not he, were the guilty one. Tamar wept loudly as she wandered the streets. When her brother Absalom found her, he hushed her, saying, "Be still now, my sister. Do not take this affair to heart." But Absalom took it to heart, hating Amnon for what he had done.

Though David was furious when he heard the news, he did nothing to punish Amnon. Absalom, however, did not share his father's hesitation. Instead, he bided his time, waiting for an opportunity for vengeance. Two years later, he murdered his half-brother Amnon.

Tamar, unprotected by her father, betrayed by her own brother, lived in Absalom's house, a desolate woman, without the possibility of marriage or children. Thus a chain of sin wove its way through David's family, enslaving the innocent along with the guilty.

# The Promise to Heal Our Hurts

Experiences like Tamar's can haunt a woman for the rest of her life. Though help is available for those who have suffered abuse, the deepest healing comes when we experience the love and acceptance God so willingly offers. His comforting spirit can be a soothing balm, the beginning of our recovery. Remarkably, he can—with time—enable us to forgive the most grievous wrongs. He can heal the most devastating hurts.

*Hear my voice when I call, O LORD;*
*    be merciful to me and answer me. . . .*
*Though my father and mother forsake me,*
*    the LORD will receive me.*

PSALM 27:7, 10


*The LORD heals the brokenhearted*
*    and binds up their wounds.*

PSALM 147:3


*    Let your hand be with me, and keep me*
*from harm so that I will be free from pain,*
*O LORD.*

1 CHRONICLES 4:10

# Rizpah

Rizpah

Rizpah

Rizpah

*Which means*

*"a hot stone*

*or coal."*

*[David] the king took . . . the two sons of . . . Rizpah, whom she had borne to Saul, together with the five sons of Saul's daughter Merab [and] . . . he handed them over to the Gibeonites, who killed and exposed them on a hill before the LORD. . . .*

*Rizpah daughter of Aiah took sackcloth and spread it out for herself on a rock. From the beginning of the harvest till the rain poured down from the heavens on the bodies, she did not let the birds of the air touch them by day or the wild animals by night. When David was told what Aiah's daughter Rizpah, Saul's concubine, had done, he went and took the bones of Saul and his son Jonathan from the citizens of Jabesh Gilead. . . . David brought the bones of Saul and his son Jonathan from there, and the bones of those who had been killed and exposed were gathered up. They buried the bones of Saul and his son Jonathan in the tomb of Saul's father Kish, at Zela in Benjamin.*

2 SAMUEL 21:8–14

## Her Character

Saul's concubine, Rizpah was the mother of Armoni and Mephibosheth. Though a woman with few rights and little power, she displayed great courage and loyalty after the death of her sons.

—⁓—

## Her Sorrow

That her only sons were executed and their bodies dishonored because of their father's crime.

—⁓—

## Her Joy

That her sons were finally given an honorable burial.

*O*ne day a woman named Rizpah stood on a hill in Israel, watching the execution of seven men. Among the dead were her own two sons, executed for their father's crime. Rizpah had been King Saul's concubine. Her connection with Saul was unfortunate, not only because of his tragic death but because he had broken an ancient loyalty oath by murdering members of a neighboring people, the Gibeonites. But her sons, not Saul, would pay the penalty for that particular sin when they were handed over to the Gibeonites by King David, along with five other of Saul's male offspring.

It is not hard to imagine Rizpah's suffering. To watch as her body convulses in sorrow. When will she turn away from the gruesome spectacle, we wonder. But instead of fleeing the scene, she faces it. She spreads sackcloth on a rock and sits down. She will not move except to protect the bodies of her sons. Her vigil will last for several months—from mid-April to early October. Rizpah will not bury her grief as long as the bodies of her sons remain unburied.

Hearing of Rizpah's loyalty and courage, King David finally ordered the remains of the executed to be buried. Rizpah couldn't bring her sons back to life. But by refusing to hide her grief, by living out her anguish in public, she gave meaning to their deaths, making the entire nation face the evil of what had happened. Because of her no one in Israel could ignore the tragic consequences that resulted from the crimes of their leader.

Her story is tragic, her response memorable. Perhaps because of her, other mothers in Israel were spared, at least for a time, a similar grief.

# The Promise to Comfort Those Who Mourn

Rizpah's tenacity is a lesson for all who are inclined to give up when the going gets tough. She mourned. She stuck out bad weather, cold, fatigue and wild animals to protect her dead sons. Finally someone in authority took notice. Her faithfulness was rewarded, and she could rest. God promises the same to us. Whatever causes us to mourn—death, harsh parents, unloving spouses, rebellious children, financial difficulties, *whatever*—God knows and will uphold and will comfort us.

*The LORD loves the just*
*and will not forsake his faithful ones.*

PSALM 37:28

*This I call to mind*
*and therefore I have hope:*
*Because of the LORD's great love we are*
*not consumed,*
*for his compassions never fail.*
*They are new every morning;*
*great is your faithfulness.*

LAMENTATIONS 3:21–23

*Blessed are those who mourn*
*for they will be comforted.*

MATTHEW 5:4

*Jesus said, "Now is your time of grief,*
*but I will see you again and you will rejoice,*
*and no one will take away your joy."*

JOHN 16:22

# Jezebel

*Which means*

*"Where is the*

*prince?"*

*Ahab told Jezebel everything Elijah had done and how he had killed all the prophets. So Jezebel sent a messenger to Elijah to say, "May the gods deal with me, be it ever so severely, if by this time tomorrow I do not make your life like that of one of them."*

*Elijah was afraid and ran for his life. . . . [He] went a day's journey into the desert. He came to a broom tree, sat down under it and prayed that he might die. "I have had enough, LORD," he said. . . .*

*Then he lay down under the tree and fell asleep. All at once an angel touched him and said, "Get up and eat." He looked around, and there by his head was a cake of bread baked over hot coals, and a jar of water. . . . So he got up and ate and drank. Strengthened by that food, he traveled . . . until he reached Horeb, the mountain of God. . . .*

*[There] the Lord said to him, "Go back the way you came, and go to the Desert of Damascus. . . . Anoint Jehu son of Nimshi king over Israel. . . .*

*Then Jehu went to Jezreel. When Jezebel heard about it, she painted her eyes, arranged her hair and looked out of a window. As Jehu entered the gate, she asked, "Have you come in peace, Zimri, you murderer of your master?" He looked up at the window and called out, "Who is on my side? Who?" Two or three eunuchs looked down at him. "Throw her down!" Jehu said. So they threw her down.*

1 KINGS 19:1–6, 8, 15–16; 2 KINGS 9:30–33

## Her Character

A religious woman, she spread idolatry throughout Israel. Powerful, cunning, and arrogant, she actively opposed God, even in the face of indisputable proofs of his sovereignty.

―⁓―

## Her Tragedy

Her arrogance led to her death.

*J*ezebel was a Phoenician princess, married to Ahab, king of the northern kingdom of Israel. A woman of great conviction and unwavering devotion, her religious ardor was directed not to the God of Israel but to pagan fertility gods. So zealous was she that she murdered Israel's prophets, replacing them with 850 of her own.

Despite her zeal, one prophet escaped her and he was the most annoying of all. Elijah defied her by predicting a lengthy drought as God's punishment for Israel's idolatry. Then, after three and a half years of the ensuing famine, he had the boldness to challenge all 850 of Jezebel's prophets to a contest. After exposing their powerlessness, God performed a miracle through Elijah, who then single-handedly rallied the people to destroy the false prophets.

Enraged, the queen sent a messenger to Elijah, vowing to kill him. But he fled south, beyond her grasp. Later, to the queen's great annoyance, the prophet showed up again to confront King Ahab: "Because you have given yourself up to doing evil in the Lord's sight, I am bringing evil upon you: I will destroy you and your queen."

Despite Elijah's warning, Jezebel continued her reign of evil and survived her husband by at least ten years until a man named Jehu came riding into town one day.

Tough as nails, Jezebel stood proudly at an upper window of her palace. With painted eyes and perfectly coifed hair, Jezebel shouted at Jehu, but he simply ignored her, challenging her servants to throw her out the window, which they promptly did.

Like helium escaping a balloon, Jezebel's anger, threats and dire warnings disappeared in an instant. Paired with Israel's worst king, she was the nation's worst queen and one of the Bible's most infamous women.

Her story highlights the fact that God is just, as well as loving. Jezebel had years in which to avail herself of God's mercy. But despite obvious miracles and repeated warnings, she was a woman who chose, instead, to harden her heart and suffer the consequences.

# The Promise of God's Justice

Jezebel's end (2 Kings 9:33–37) is exactly what Elijah had prophesied (1 Kings 21:23). Judgment for her wicked life, when it came, was swift and sure. It's hard to reconcile this aspect of our God with our image of him as loving and compassionate. Yet how could a good God ignore the evil that Jezebel had committed? How could he have looked the other way as she inflicted terrible suffering on others? Justice, too, is a great blessing in our lives. Because God hates evil, he will surely punish it. Unless those who do evil come to him for forgiveness and reconciliation, his mercy will elude them.

*Those who cling to worthless idols*
*forfeit the grace that could be theirs.*

JONAH 2:8


*Where sin increased, grace increased all*
*the more.*

ROMANS 5:20


*We implore you on Christ's behalf: Be*
*reconciled to God. God made Jesus who had*
*no sin to be sin for us, so that in him we*
*might become the righteousness of God.*

2 CORINTHIANS 5:20–21


*This is what the Sovereign LORD, the*
*Holy One of Israel, says:*
*"In repentance and rest is your salvation."*

ISAIAH 30:15

# Widow of Zarephath

*Her flour and*

*oil did not*

*run out.*

Then the word of the LORD came to [Elijah]: "Go at once to Zarephath of Sidon and stay there. I have commanded a widow in that place to supply you with food." So he went to Zarephath. When he came to the town gate, a widow was there gathering sticks. He called to her and asked, "Would you . . . bring me, please, a piece of bread."

"As surely as the LORD your God lives," she replied, "I don't have any bread—only a handful of flour in a jar and a little oil in a jug. I am gathering a few sticks to take home and make a meal for myself and my son, that we may eat it— and die."

Elijah said to her, "Don't be afraid. Go home and do as you have said. But first make a small cake of bread for me from what you have and bring it to me, and then make something for yourself and your son. For this is what the LORD, the God of Israel, says: 'The jar of flour will not be used up and the jug of oil will not run dry until the day the LORD gives rain on the land.'"

She went away and did as Elijah had told her. So there was food every day for Elijah and for the woman and her family.

1 KINGS 17:8–15

## Her Character

Facing starvation in the midst of the long drought that Elijah had predicted, she showed extraordinary hospitality to one of God's prophets, providing a safe harbor for him.

---

## Her Sorrow

To suffer extreme poverty, famine, and the loss of her husband.

---

## Her Joy

To experience repeated miracles of God's provision.

*H*er arms were spindly and rough, like the dry twigs she gathered for kindling. Every night she hoped for rain, but every morning she woke to a brilliant sky. Though she starved herself to feed her child, his distended belly accused her. His need condemned her. She had failed in the most basic way a mother could, unable to protect, nurture and provide for her child. Now she would prepare a final supper for herself and her son.

But as she was gathering sticks for the fire, a stranger called out to her: "Please bring me water to drink."

As she went to fetch it, he called after her, "Please bring along a bit of bread."

Astonished at such a request, she replied, "As the Lord, your God, lives, I have nothing baked; there is only a handful of flour in my jar and a little oil in my jug. Just now I was going to prepare something for myself and my son; when we have eaten it, we shall die."

But the stranger persisted. "Do not be afraid. Go and do as you propose. But bring me a little cake. For the Lord, the God of Israel, says, 'The jar of flour shall not go empty, nor the jug of oil run dry, until the day when the Lord sends rain upon the earth.'"

Remarkably, she did exactly as he asked, feeding him the food she had reserved for herself and her son.

The woman from Zarephath wasn't a Jew but a Phoenician. She must have felt utterly alone, not realizing that God would provide miraculously for her and her child. In truth, she lacked everything but the one thing she needed most—a commodity of the heart called faith.

Because of God's miraculous act, her life and her son's life were spared. Every time she dipped her hand into the flour and every time she poured oil from the jug, she saw a miracle unfold. Just as Elijah had promised, the supply of flour and oil lasted, never failing until at last the rains came and revived the land.

# The Promise of Provision

God doesn't ignore the needs of those who cannot help themselves. He doesn't urge them to pick themselves up and get going when they have no resources to do so. He doesn't pat them on the back and say he's sorry life is so tough. Instead, he sometimes intervenes with miraculous understatement, in this case by making sure that a little bit of oil and flour—just enough for a small loaf—didn't run out. Our God still provides for us, granting what we need in some unexpected ways.

*From your bounty, O God, you provided*
*for the poor.*

PSALM 68:10

*God provides food for those who fear him;*
*he remembers his covenant forever.*

PSALM 111:5

*Put [your] hope in God, who richly*
*provides us with everything for our*
*enjoyment.*

1 TIMOTHY 6:17

*You gave abundant showers, O God;*
*you refreshed your weary inheritance.*

PSALM 68:9

# The
# Shunammite
# Woman

The Shunammite
Woman

The Shunammite
Woman

The Shunammite
Woman

*Her hospitality*

*brought great*

*rewards and a*

*wonderful miracle.*

One day Elisha went to Shunem. And a well-to-do woman was there, who urged him to stay for a meal. So whenever he came by, he stopped there to eat. She said to her husband, "I know that this man who often comes our way is a holy man of God. Let's make a small room on the roof and put in it a bed and a table, a chair and a lamp for him. Then he can stay there whenever he comes to us." . . .

Elisha said to [his servant], "Tell [the Shunammite woman], 'You have gone to all this trouble for us. Now what can be done for you? Can we speak on your behalf to the king or the commander of the army?'" She replied, "I have a home among my own people."

"What can be done for her?" Elisha asked [his servant]. Gehazi said, "Well, she has no son and her husband is old."

Then Elisha said [to her], "You will hold a son in your arms." . . . The next year about that same time she gave birth to a son, just as Elisha had told her.

The child grew, and one day he . . . died. . . .

When Elisha reached the house, there was the boy lying dead on his couch. He went in, shut the door on the two of them and prayed to the LORD. . . . The boy sneezed seven times and opened his eyes.

2 KINGS 4:8–10; 13–18, 20, 32–33, 35

## Her Character

Generous and hospitable, she was a wealthy and capable woman, who showed great kindness to one of God's prophets.

---

## Her Sorrow

To lose the son that had been promised her.

---

## Her Joy

To experience just how deep God's faithfulness goes.

*A* wealthy Jewish woman invited the prophet Elisha to linger for a meal at her home in Shunem. Afterward, she said to her husband, "Let us arrange a little room on the roof and furnish it for him, so that when he comes to us he can stay there."

Moved by her kindness, Elisha inquired, through his servant Gehazi, whether he could use his influence with Israel's king on her behalf. But the woman wasn't looking for favors at court, so Elisha pressed his servant, "What, then, can be done for her?"

Gehazi merely pointed out the obvious: the woman and her aging husband were childless. So Elisha summoned the woman and promised her: "This time next year you will be holding a baby son." Overcome by Elisha's prophecy, the woman begged him not to deceive her. But a year later, just as Elisha had foretold, she held an infant in her arms.

One morning a servant entered the house with the little boy in his arms, explaining that the child had complained of a headache while visiting his father in the fields. Perhaps he had lingered too long in the sun.

The boy's face was flushed, his forehead hot as she caressed it. His breathing was labored, his eyes listless. At about noon he died.

Without a word, she carried his small body to the prophet's room, laying it tenderly on Elisha's bed. Closing the door, she summoned a servant and left immediately to find Elisha.

As soon as she saw him, she exclaimed: "Did I ask my lord for a son? Did I not beg you not to deceive me?"

So the prophet hurried back to Shunem. He found the boy cold on his couch. Praying, Elisha stretched his body across the boy's. As he lay there, he could feel the small body warming beneath him. He got up and paced the room, then again stretched himself across the lifeless body and prayed. The boy sneezed! Then sneezed again.

Overcome by the miracle, the grateful mother fell at Elisha's feet. God had been true to his word, fulfilling his promise to her and then preserving it in the face of impossible circumstances.

# The Promise of God's Faithfulness

The Shunammite woman knew God was faithful even when she experienced the most devastating of circumstances, the death of her little son. Her son was gone, but the God who had given him to her wasn't gone. She knew he hadn't forsaken her.

Can you trust in God's faithfulness even when it seems like your world is crashing in on you? It's difficult. But remember that even in the most agonizing of circumstances, even when you feel abandoned, even when tragedy strikes—God is there.

*God is not a man, that he should lie,*
*nor a son of man, that he should*
*change his mind.*
*Does he speak and then not act?*
*Does he promise and not fulfill?*

NUMBERS 23:19


*No matter how many promises God has*
*made, they are "Yes" in Christ.*

2 CORINTHIANS 1:20


*Let us hold unswervingly to the hope we*
*profess, for God who promised is faithful.*

HEBREWS 10:23

# The Wise Woman of Abel

The Wise Woman
of Abel

The Wise Woman
of Abel

*She acted*

*with wisdom*

*to save*

*her city.*

Sheba passed through all the tribes of Israel to Abel Beth Maacah. . . . All the troops with Joab came and besieged Sheba in Abel Beth Maacah. They built a siege ramp up to the city, and it stood against the outer fortifications. While they were battering the wall to bring it down, a wise woman called from the city, "Listen! Listen! Tell Joab to come here so I can speak to him." He went toward her, and she asked, "Are you Joab?"

"I am," he answered.

She said, "Listen to what your servant has to say."

"I'm listening," he said. . . .

She continued, . . . "We are the peaceful and faithful in Israel. You are trying to destroy a city that is a mother in Israel. Why do you want to swallow up the LORD's inheritance?"

"Far be it from me!" Joab replied, "Far be it from me to swallow up or destroy! That is not the case. A man named Sheba son of Bicri, from the hill country of Ephraim, has lifted up his hand against the king, against David. Hand over this one man, and I'll withdraw from the city."

The woman said to Joab, "His head will be thrown to you from the wall."

Then the woman went to all the people with her wise advice, and they cut off the head of Sheba son of Bicri and threw it to Joab. So he sounded the trumpet, and his men dispersed from the city, each returning to his home. And Joab went back to the king in Jerusalem.

## Her Character

Rather than passively waiting for someone else to save her city, she had the wisdom and courage to act quickly and decisively.

―⁓―

## Her Sorrow

That a rebellious leader had infiltrated her city.

―⁓―

## Her Joy

That she was able to successfully intercede for the town, thus averting disaster for many innocent people.

*M*any women in Scripture stand out for their wisdom. One woman, who lived in a town at Israel's northern border, is identified solely as "a wise woman" (2 Samuel 20:16), acting quickly to save her city.

In the midst of political instability late in David's reign, a rabble-rouser by the name of Sheba led a revolt against the king. Joab, the commander of David's army, chased him all the way to Abel Beth Maacah in the northern regions of Israel.

Joab had constructed siege ramps to assault the walls of the city and squelch the rebellion. It was evident the entire city would be destroyed unless someone acted quickly to preserve the peace.

Suddenly, a woman stood on the walls of Abel and shouted: "Listen! Listen! We are the peaceful and faithful in Israel," she cried out. "You are trying to destroy a city that is a mother in Israel. Why do you want to swallow up the Lord's inheritance?" she challenged Joab.

"Far be it from me to swallow up or destroy!" he replied. "A man named

Sheba has lifted up his hand against King David. Hand over this one man, and I'll withdraw from the city."

"His head will be thrown to you from the wall," she shouted back.

So the woman turned to her fellow citizens, urging them to act. In just moments, a man's head came careening over the wall. Innocent lives on both sides of the city walls were spared because one woman acted wisely and well, interceding on behalf of her people.

The men in the story appear to behave only in conventional terms. Mobilize the army, build a siege ramp, violently smash the city walls and squelch the rebellion. But the woman looked for another solution, one that would keep the peace and save lives. Her courage in speaking up and acting quickly brought peace to a situation that had seemed hopeless just moments before.

## The Blessing of Wisdom

Though the story is a violent one it is yet a story of peace, because the woman's quick action spared the lives of many innocent people. Though wisdom may make its appearance in surprising ways, it always brings blessing, supporting what is right and protecting the innocent.

*Wisdom makes one wise man more*
    *powerful than ten rulers in a city.*

*The LORD gives wisdom,*
    *and from his mouth come knowledge*
    *and understanding.*
*He holds victory in store for the upright,*
    *he is a shield to those whose walk is*
    *blameless.*

PROVERBS 2:6–7

*[A noble woman] speaks with wisdom,*
    *and faithful instruction is on her*
    *tongue. . . .*
*Charm is deceptive, and beauty is fleeting;*
    *but a woman who fears the LORD is*
    *to be praised.*
*Give her the reward she has earned,*
    *and let her works bring her praise at*
    *the city gate.*

PROVERBS 31:26, 30–31

x

Gomer

Gomer

Gomer

Gomer

*Which means*

*"completion."*

*When the LORD began to speak through Hosea, the LORD said to him, "Go, take to yourself an adulterous wife and children of unfaithfulness, because the land is guilty of the vilest adultery in departing from the LORD." So he married Gomer. . . .*

*Rebuke your mother, rebuke her, for she is not my wife, and I am not her husband. Let her remove the adulterous look from her face and the unfaithfulness from between her breasts. . . . I will not show my love to her children, because they are the children of adultery. Their mother has been unfaithful and has conceived them in disgrace. She said, 'I will go after my lovers, who give me my food and my water, my wool and my linen, my oil and my drink.' . . . Then she will say, 'I will go back to my husband as at first, for then I was better off than now.' . . .*

*The LORD said to me, "Go, show your love to your wife again, though she is loved by another and is an adulteress. Love her as the LORD loves the Israelites, though they turn to other gods and love the sacred raisin cakes."*

*So I bought her for fifteen shekels of silver and about a homer and a lethek of barley. Then I told her, "You are to live with me many days; you must not be a prostitute or be intimate with any man, and I will live with you."*

HOSEA 1:2–3; 2:2, 4–5, 7; 3:1–3

## Her Character

Though a married woman, she carried on numerous love affairs, crediting her lovers for the gifts her husband had given her.

---

## Her Sorrow

To have become the symbol of spiritual adultery—a picture of Israel's unfaithfulness to God.

---

## Her Joy

That her husband continued to love her despite her unfaithfulness.

*T*he man stood at the door, craning his neck and peering through the half-light. Other than a stray dog curled in a knot against the wall of a neighboring house, he saw nothing. It was too late for a woman to be walking the streets alone. But, then, she wouldn't be alone, would she?

By noon tomorrow, the news of her betrayal would start tongues wagging all over town. Hosea, the man who would steer the nation with his prophecies, couldn't even control his own wife.

But hadn't God instructed him: "Go, take to yourself an adulterous wife and children of unfaithfulness, because the land is guilty of the vilest adultery in departing from the Lord." And so Hosea married Gomer and named his children Jezreel (*God Scatters*), Lo-Ruhamah (*Not Loved*), and Lo-Ammi (*Not My People*). Each successive child measured the growing rift between husband and wife.

The word of the Lord that had filled Hosea's mouth now troubled his soul. So this was how God felt about his own people—bitterly betrayed, cut to the heart, outraged. His tender love meant nothing to a people enamored with Canaanite gods.

If only Israel would learn its lesson and turn back to the Lord—if only Gomer would turn back. Hosea wanted to shout in her face, shake her awake to her sin. Enough of patience. Enough of tenderness. She had ignored his threats. What choice had he now? He would shame her, punishing her unfaithfulness.

In the midst of his bitter grief, he heard a surprising command from God, instructing him to take back his wife, loving her as the Lord loved the people of Israel. So Hosea took Gomer back. And the word of the Lord transformed Lo-Ruhamah into Ruhamah (*Loved*) and Lo-Ammi into Ammi (*My People*).

The story of Gomer and Hosea is a poignant portrayal of God's jealous love for his people. But this is a tangled love story, in which God's heart is repeatedly broken as his people turn away from him toward idols. The lives of Hosea and Gomer were a living reminder to the Israelites of both God's judgment and his love.

# The Promise of God's Love

Gomer's story is an ugly little tale with a beautiful message. A tempestuous marriage. A wife who will not remain faithful to the husband who loves her. A husband who not only remains faithful, but loving. Children whose paternity is in doubt. All these are the elements not of a soap opera but of a picture of God's love and faithfulness to his often unloving and unfaithful people. God loves us and remains faithful to us even when we abandon him and turn away. He waits. His arms are open. He only asks our repentance and his blessings will again overflow.

*I will give them a heart to know me, that I am the LORD. They will be my people, and I will be their God, for they will return to me with all their heart.*

JEREMIAH 24: 7

*Repent, then, and turn to God, so that your sins may be wiped out, that times of refreshing may come from the Lord.*

ACTS 3:19

*How great is the love the Father has lavished on us, that we should be called children of God!*

1 JOHN 3:1

*"I will betroth you to me forever; I will betroth you in righteousness and justice, in love and compassion," says the Lord.*

HOSEA 2:19

Elizabeth

*Which means*

*"God is*

*my oath."*

*[Zechariah and Elizabeth] had no children, because Elizabeth was barren; and they were both well along in years.*

*Once when Zechariah's division was on duty and he was serving as priest before God . . . an angel of the Lord appeared to him, standing at the right side of the altar of incense. . . . The angel said to him: "Do not be afraid, Zechariah. . . . Your wife Elizabeth will bear you a son, and you are to give him the name John. He will be a joy and delight to you, and many will rejoice because of his birth." . . .*

*Elizabeth became pregnant and for five months remained in seclusion. "The Lord has done this for me," she said. "In these days he has shown his favor and taken away my disgrace among the people." . . .*

*Mary got ready and hurried to a town in the hill country of Judea, where she entered Zechariah's home and greeted Elizabeth. When Elizabeth heard Mary's greeting, the baby leaped in her womb, and Elizabeth was filled with the Holy Spirit. In a loud voice she exclaimed: "Blessed are you among women, and blessed is the child you will bear! But why am I so favored, that the mother of my Lord should come to me? As soon as the sound of your greeting reached my ears, the baby in my womb leaped for joy. Blessed is she who has believed that what the Lord has said to her will be accomplished!"*

Luke 1:7–8, 11, 13–14, 24–25, 39–45

## Her Character

A descendant of Aaron, Elizabeth was a woman the Bible calls "righteous in the eyes of God." Like very few others, male or female, she is praised for observing all the Lord's commandments and regulations without blame. She is the first to acknowledge Jesus as Lord.

## Her Sorrow

To be barren for most of her life.

## Her Joy

To give birth to John, later known as John the Baptist, the Messiah's forerunner. His name, divinely assigned, meant, "the Lord is gracious."

*E*lizabeth's eyes winked out at the world from cheeks that had baked too long in the sun. Snowy strands of hair straggled from beneath a woolen shawl. Small hands rested tenderly on her rounded belly, softly probing for any hint of movement. But all was still. She and Zechariah had been content enough in their quiet house these last few months, secluded in their joy. Sometimes she shook with laughter as she thought about how God had rearranged her life—planting a child in her old-woman's womb.

From her vantage point on the roof of the house, she noticed a young girl walking up the pathway and wondered who her visitor might be. The older woman stepped carefully down the stairs and into the house to welcome her guest. But with the young woman's words of greeting came something that felt like a gale force wind. Steadying herself, the older woman felt suddenly invigorated. Her unborn baby leapt inside her as she shouted out a welcoming response: "Blessed are you among women, and blessed is the child you will bear! But why am I so favored, that the mother of my Lord should come to me? As soon as the sound of your greeting reached my ears, the baby in my womb leaped for joy. Blessed is she who has believed that what the Lord has said to her will be accomplished."

Mary had made the journey all the way from Nazareth to visit her relative, Elizabeth. An angel had whispered the secret of the older woman's pregnancy to the virgin, who was also with child.

The two women held each other, their bonds of kinship now so much stronger than what mere flesh and blood could forge. For Israel's God was on the move again, bringing the long-ago promise to fulfillment. And blessed was she who did not doubt that what the Lord had said to her would be accomplished.

# The Promise of a Savior

God always keeps his promises! For hundreds of years, God had been telling the people of Israel that he would send a Messiah who would provide a direct bridge to God himself, one whose sacrifice would provide redemption for all time. The events in this first chapter of Luke are just the beginning of the fulfillment of God's greatest promise to his people. God hasn't forgotten! With Elizabeth we can say: *"The Lord has done this for me!"*

*Zechariah . . . prophesied:*
*"And you, my child, will be called a*
 *prophet of the Most High;*
 *for you will go on before the Lord to*
  *prepare the way for him,*
*to give his people the knowledge of*
 *salvation*
 *through the forgiveness of their sins,*
*because of the tender mercy of our God,*
 *by which the rising sun will come to us*
  *from heaven*
*to shine on those living in darkness*
 *and in the shadow of death,*
*to guide our feet into the path of peace."*

LUKE 1:67, 76-79

*To us a child is born*
 *to us a son is given,*
 *and the government will be on his*
  *shoulders.*
*And he will be called*
 *Wonderful Counselor, Mighty God,*
 *Everlasting Father, Prince of Peace.*

ISAIAH 9:6

 *The virgin will be with child and will*
*give birth to a son, and they will call him*
*"Immanuel"—which means, "God with us."*

MATTHEW 1:23

# The Woman of Samaria

The Woman
of Samaria

The Woman
of Samaria

The Woman
of Samaria

*She drank of*

*living water.*

*When a Samaritan woman came to draw water, Jesus said to her, "Will you give me a drink?"* . . .

*[She] said to him, "You are a Jew and I am a Samaritan woman. How can you ask me for a drink?" (For Jews do not associate with Samaritans.)*

*Jesus answered her, "If you knew the gift of God and who it is that asks you for a drink, you would have asked him and he would have given you living water."* . . . *"Everyone who drinks this water will be thirsty again, but whoever drinks the water I give him will never thirst. Indeed, the water I give him will become in him a spring of water welling up to eternal life."*

*The woman said to him, "Sir, give me this water so that I won't get thirsty and have to keep coming here to draw water."* . . .

*He told her, "Go, call your husband and come back."*

*"I have no husband," she replied.*

*Jesus said to her, "You are right when you say you have no husband. The fact is, you have had five husbands, and the man you now have is not your husband."*

*"Sir," the woman said, ". . . I know that Messiah" (called Christ) "is coming. . . ."*

*Then Jesus declared, "I who speak to you am he."* . . .

*Then the woman went back to the town . . . Many of the Samaritans from that town believed in him because of the woman's testimony.*

JOHN 4:7, 9–10, 13–19, 25–26, 28, 39

## Her Character

The Jews would have looked down on her because she was a Samaritan. Men would have discounted her because she was a woman. And women would have disdained her because of her many romantic liaisons. She would not have been most people's first choice to advance the gospel in a region where it had not yet been heard.

---

## Her Sorrow

To have lived in a way that probably relegated her to the margins of society.

---

## Her Joy

That Jesus broke through barriers of culture, race, gender and religion in order to reveal himself to her.

*E*very day, the woman carried her water jug to Jacob's well. Though it was the hottest time of the day, she preferred it to the evening hours, when the other women gathered. How tired she was of their gossiping tongues. Better the scorching heat than listening to their sharp remarks about her.

She was surprised, however, to see that today someone had already arrived at the well. At least she had nothing to fear from his tongue, for Jews avoided Samaritans. But as she approached the well, the man startled her, breaking the rules she had counted on to protect her.

"Will you give me a drink?" he said.

With a toss of her head, she replied, "You are a Jew and I am a Samaritan woman. How can you ask me for a drink?"

But he wouldn't be put off. "If you knew the gift of God and who it is that asks you for a drink, you would have asked him and he would have given you living water. Go, call your husband and come back."

Her normally quick tongue was barely able to reply, "I do not have a husband."

"You are right," Jesus replied. "You have had five husbands, and the one you have now is not your husband."

His words cut her. She tried changing the subject. "I know that the Messiah is coming. When he comes, he will tell us everything."

Then Jesus declared, "I who speak to you am he."

Leaving her water jar, the woman went back to the town and said to the people, "Come see a man who told me everything I have done. Could he possibly be the Messiah?"

Dodge, counter dodge—nothing the woman said would keep Jesus at bay. He pressed beneath the surface, hemming her in by revealing his knowledge of the most intimate details of her life. Overwhelmed, she finally admitted the truth. And when she did, Jesus startled her with a revelation about himself. He admitted, for the first time, that he was the Messiah. As a result of his encounter with the woman of Samaria, many Samaritans came to believe in him.

# The Promise of Fulfillment

Are you thirsty? Is there a longing in you that you just can't seem to satisfy? Do you hunger for something to fill some void, some emptiness that you can't even explain? Look everywhere, try everything, but you'll find nothing in this world that will satisfy. Only Jesus can provide the living water that will fill you to overflowing, that will satisfy your every longing, that will soothe your thirst so completely that you'll never be thirsty again.

*Satisfy us in the morning with your*
  *unfailing love, O LORD,*
    *that we may sing for joy and be glad*
    *all our days.*

PSALM 90:14


*Blessed are those who hunger and thirst*
  *for righteousness,*
  *for they will be filled.*

MATTHEW 5:6


*Jesus said, "Everyone who drinks this*
*water will be thirsty again, but whoever*
*drinks the water I give him will never thirst.*
*Indeed, the water I give him will become in*
*him a spring of water welling up to eternal*
*life."*

JOHN 4:13–14

# The Woman Who Lived a Sinful Life

The Woman Who
Lived a Sinful Life

The Woman Wh
Lived a Sinful Lif

*Forgiven much,*

*she loved much.*

*Now one of the Pharisees [Simon] invited Jesus to have dinner with him, so he went to the Pharisee's house and reclined at the table. When a woman who had lived a sinful life in that town learned that Jesus was eating at the Pharisee's house, she brought an alabaster jar of perfume, and as she stood behind him at his feet weeping, she began to wet his feet with her tears. Then she wiped them with her hair, kissed them and poured perfume on them. . . .*

*Then Jesus turned toward the woman and said to Simon, "Do you see this woman? I came into your house. You did not give me any water for my feet, but she wet my feet with her tears and wiped them with her hair. You did not give me a kiss, but this woman, from the time I entered, has not stopped kissing my feet. You did not put oil on my head, but she has poured perfume on my feet. Therefore, I tell you, her many sins have been forgiven—for she loved much. But he who has been forgiven little loves little."*

LUKE 7:36–38, 44–47

# Her Character

She was a notorious sinner, most likely a prostitute. Rather than trying to defend what was indefensible in her life, she admitted her sin and made a spectacle of herself in a passionate display of love and gratitude.

---

# Her Sorrow

That she had offended God so grievously.

---

# Her Joy

That Jesus forgave her sins and commended her for her great faith and love.

*T*he woman felt as though her world had altered in a moment's time. The weight of an unhappy future had suddenly been lifted from her shoulders. She felt clean and whole as she followed the rabbi through the doorway of Simon's house.

Ignoring the stares of the men, she went to where Jesus was reclining at table. She hardly knew what she was doing as she bent down and covered his feet with her kisses and then anointed them with precious perfume, wiping his feet with her hair. How else could she express her heart to the man who had loved her so well?

---

Simon the Pharisee loved the law better than anything or anyone. It was like a fence that safeguarded his sense of security. He watched the scene unfold, surprised that a prostitute would even enter his house. "If this man were a prophet," Simon thought, "he would know what sort of woman is touching him, that she is a sinner."

As though he had overheard Simon's secret thoughts, Jesus turned and spoke to him, telling him a parable about two people who had been forgiven a debt. Then he said, "Do you see this woman? She has bathed my feet with her tears and wiped them with her hair. She has not ceased kissing my feet since the time I entered. I tell you, her many sins have been forgiven. But the one who has been forgiven little loves little."

Then Jesus said to the woman. "Your sins are forgiven; go in peace."

———

Though the woman was a notorious sinner, she recognized her great need for grace. Repentance turned her world on its head. Simon, by contrast, was a religious man whose habit of judging others shielded his neat and orderly life from the unpredictable power of grace.

Simon and the woman both owed a debt they could not possibly repay. Though his sin was less obvious, it was the more dangerous. He was like a man who was following a map he was certain would lead to heaven. But when heaven came down and walked into his house, he didn't even know it. The woman, on the other hand, realized just how lost she had been. Forgiven much, she loved much. She found heaven at the feet of Jesus.

# The Promise of Forgiveness

Let's admit it, many of us would respond to this sinful woman just as the Pharisee did. It's easy to look at people whose lives have been devastated by sin with more judgment than love. But Jesus looked at her *and* at Simon and saw the same thing: their need for forgiveness. And he gave it freely. We don't know what Simon's ultimate response was, but the woman's response is evident in her tears and kisses. She went away forgiven. This story is included in the Bible so we can know that no matter how sinful, how broken, how entrenched in error we might be, forgiveness is available.

*When we were overwhelmed by sins,*
*    you forgave our transgressions, O Lord.*

PSALM 65:3


*You are forgiving and good, O Lord,*
*    abounding in love to all who call to you.*

PSALM 86:5


*In Christ we have redemption through*
*his blood, the forgiveness of sins, in accordance*
*with the riches of God's grace that he*
*lavished on us.*

EPHESIANS 1: 7-8

# The Woman
# who was
# Healed

The Woman who
was Healed

The Woman who
was Healed

*She was healed*

*with a touch.*

*A large crowd followed and pressed around Jesus. And a woman was there who had been subject to bleeding for twelve years. She had suffered a great deal under the care of many doctors and had spent all she had, yet instead of getting better she grew worse. When she heard about Jesus, she came up behind him in the crowd and touched his cloak, because she thought, "If I just touch his clothes, I will be healed." Immediately her bleeding stopped and she felt in her body that she was freed from her suffering.*

*At once Jesus realized that power had gone out from him. He turned around in the crowd and asked, "Who touched my clothes?"*

*"You see the people crowding against you," his disciples answered, "and yet you can ask, 'Who touched me?'"*

*But Jesus kept looking around to see who had done it. Then the woman, knowing what had happened to her, came and fell at his feet and, trembling with fear, told him the whole truth. He said to her, "Daughter, your faith has healed you. Go in peace and be freed from your suffering."*

MARK 5:24–34

## Her Character

She was so desperate for healing that she ignored the conventions of the day for the chance to touch Jesus.

—⁓—

## Her Sorrow

To have suffered a chronic illness that isolated her from others for twelve years.

—⁓—

## Her Joy

That after long years of suffering, she finally found peace and freedom.

*T*he woman hovered at the edge of the crowd. Nobody noticed as she melted into the throng of bodies. Nobody recoiled from her touch. She pressed closer, but a noisy swarm of men still blocked her view. Suddenly the group in front of her parted. It was all she needed.

Her arm darted through the opening, fingers brushing his cloak. Instantly, she felt a warmth spread through her, flushing out the pain, clearing out the decay. Her skin prickled and shivered. She felt strong and able, like a young girl coming into her own

Before she could disappear into the crowd, Jesus blocked her escape and silenced the people around him with a curious question: "Who touched me?"

"Who touched him? He must be joking!" voices murmured. "People are shoving just to get near him!"

Shaking now, the woman fell at Jesus' feet: "For twelve years, I have been bleeding. I have spent all my money on doctors but only grown worse. I knew that if I could just touch your garment,

I would be healed." But touching, she knew, meant spreading her defilement—even to the rabbi.

Twelve years of loneliness. Twelve years in which physicians had bled her of all her wealth. Her private affliction a matter of public record. Every cup she handled, every chair she sat on could transmit her defilement to others. Even though her impurity was considered a ritual matter rather than an ethical one, it had rendered her an outcast.

But instead of scolding and shaming her for touching him, Jesus praised her: "Daughter, your faith has saved you. Go in peace."

His words must have been like water breaching a dam, breaking through her isolation, setting her free. That day, countless men and women had brushed against Jesus, but only one had truly touched him. And instead of being defiled by contact with her, his own touch had proven the more contagious, rendering her pure and whole again.

# The Promise of Healing

God promises to heal us. That statement may seem to fly in the face of the many who have suffered from illness and disability for years on end. But our concept of healing is not necessarily the same as God's. For some, healing may not take place here on earth. But true healing—the healing that will cure even those who don't suffer from any particular physical ailment—will take place not here but in heaven. There, God promises the ultimate healing from our sickness, our disabilities, our bent toward sinning.

*I am the LORD, who heals you.*

EXODUS 15:26

*O LORD my God, I called to you for help and you healed me.*

PSALM 30:2

*They will be his people, and God himself will be with them and be their God. He will wipe every tear from their eyes. There will be no more death or mourning or crying or pain, for the old order of things has passed away.*

REVELATION 21:3–4

*Praise the LORD, O my soul,
    and forget not all his benefits—
who forgives all your sins
    and heals all your diseases.*

PSALM 103:2–3

# Herodias

Herodias

Herodias

Herodias

*The female*

*form of Herod,*

*which means*

*"heroic."*

*Now Herod had arrested John and bound him and put him in prison because of Herodias, his brother Philip's wife, for John had been saying to him: "It is not lawful for you to have her." Herod wanted to kill John, but he was afraid of the people, because they considered him a prophet.*

*On Herod's birthday the daughter of Herodias danced for them and pleased Herod so much that he promised with an oath to give her whatever she asked. Prompted by her mother, she said, "Give me here on a platter the head of John the Baptist." The king was distressed, but because of his oaths and his dinner guests, he ordered that her request be granted and had John beheaded in the prison. His head was brought in on a platter and given to the girl, who carried it to her mother. John's disciples came and took his body and buried it. Then they went and told Jesus.*

MATTHEW 14:3–12

## Her Character

A proud woman, she used her daughter to manipulate her husband into doing her will.

---

## Her Shame

To be rebuked by an upstart prophet for leaving her husband Philip in order to marry his half-brother Herod Antipas.

*H*erodias's grandfather had ruled Judea for thirty-four years. Though Herod the Great had brought stability to a troubled region of the Roman Empire, his reign contained shadows that darkened as the years went on. He had slaughtered Jewish infants in Bethlehem, and murdered his favorite wife and three of his sons. Herodias's husband, Philip, and his half brother Herod Antipas, both sons of Herod the Great, had been lucky survivors of his paranoia.

After a while, Herodias tired of Philip and divorced him to marry Herod Antipas. Though their unlawful marriage alienated their Jewish subjects, neither Herod nor Herodias, expected their transgression to become a matter of public agitation. But trouble was edging toward them in the form of a prophet who cared nothing for diplomacy. John the Baptist was a man who was fearlessly preaching the need for repentance. He spared no one, not even Herod Antipas, whom he reproached for marrying his brother's wife.

Herodias must have been pleased when her husband imprisoned John but upset that he hadn't done more to silence him. For even Herod had to step carefully, lest he ignite an uprising among John's ever-growing number of followers.

On Herod's birthday a feast was held in his honor. During the evening, Herodias's young daughter, Salome, performed a dance for Herod and his guests, which so pleased him that he promised his stepdaughter anything she desired, up to half his kingdom.

Ever the good daughter, Salome hastened to her mother for advice. When Salome returned to the banquet hall, she surprised Herod with a gruesome demand: "Give me the head of John the Baptist on a platter."

Though Herod was distressed by her request, he was even more distressed at the prospect of breaking an oath he had so publicly made. Therefore, in complete disregard for Jewish law, which prohibited execution without trial and decapitation as a form of execution, he immediately ordered John's death.

# The Blessing of Cleansing

As negative as it sounds, the lesson or promise learned from Herodias can only be that sin will devour us. If sin always has its way in our lives, it will eventually consume us. There is only one way out: If we abandon our sin and repent, we will find forgiveness and a new life in Christ. Jesus promises to pardon even the most horrific sins, the most depraved lifestyles, the most abandoned behaviors. His forgiveness consumes the sin. We may still face its consequences, but we will no longer have to fear its judgment. Before God, with Christ as our mediator, we are as if we had never sinned.

*If you, O LORD, kept a record of sins,*
 *O Lord, who could stand?*
*But with you there is forgiveness.*

PSALM 130:3–4


*"Come now, let us reason together,"*
 *says the LORD.*
*"Though your sins are like scarlet,*
 *they shall be as white as snow;*
*though they are red as crimson,*
 *they shall be like wool."*

ISAIAH 1:18


*Because of his great love for us, God, who*
*is rich in mercy, made us alive with Christ*
*even when we were dead in transgressions—*
*it is by grace you have been saved.*

EPHESIANS 2:4–5

Joanna

Joanna

Joanna

Joanna

*Which means*

*"the Lord is*

*gracious."*

Jesus traveled about from one town and village to another, proclaiming the good news of the kingdom of God. The Twelve were with him, and also some women who had been cured of evil spirits and diseases: Mary (called Magdalene) from whom seven demons had come out; Joanna the wife of Cuza, the manager of Herod's household; Susanna; and many others. These women were helping to support them out of their own means. . . .

With loud shouts [the Jews] insistently demanded that [Jesus] be crucified, and their shouts prevailed. . . . They came to the place called the Skull, there they crucified him. . . .

Jesus called out with a loud voice, "Father, into your hands I commit my spirit." When he had said this, he breathed his last. . . .

On the first day of the week, very early in the morning, the women took the spices they had prepared and went to the tomb. They found the stone rolled away from the tomb, but when they entered, they did not find the body of the Lord Jesus. While they were wondering about this, suddenly two men in clothes that gleamed like lightning stood beside them. In their fright the women bowed down with their faces to the ground, but the men said to them, "Why do you look for the living among the dead? He is not here; he has risen!"

LUKE 8:1–3; 23:23, 33, 46; 24:1–6

## Her Character

A woman of high rank in Herod's court, she experienced healing at Jesus' hands. She responded by giving herself totally, supporting his ministry and following him wherever he went. The story of her healing may have been known to Herod himself.

---

## Her Sorrow

To watch her Savior die.

---

## Her Joy

To find the tomb empty except for the angels who proclaimed that Jesus was alive.

*J*oanna was a wealthy woman, accustomed to an atmosphere of worldliness. One didn't live in Herod's courts without learning to navigate the powerful currents of intrigue that swirled continuously around his throne. But nothing had so troubled and sickened her as the death of the prophet John. How sad she had been as she watched Jesus grieving his cousin's murder.

Joanna's own life had been so altered by Christ that she may have hoped to influence Herod on his behalf. Married to Cuza, the manager of Herod's vast estates, she was well positioned for the task. But after John's death, Joanna must have wondered what would become of Jesus should he ever have the misfortune of falling into Herod's hands. And what, for that matter, would become of his followers?

Though Joanna would have realized the escalating risks that faith required, there is not the slightest evidence that she flinched from them. Whether her faith cost her dearly or little in either her marriage or at court is a matter for speculation.

We do know, however, that Joanna provided for Jesus' needs from her own purse and that she was present at the resurrection along with Mary Magdalene and Mary the mother of James. Like the others who went to the tomb to anoint Jesus' body, Joanna fell on her face in awe of the angels who greeted her with astonishing news:"Why do you look for the living among the dead? He is not here; he has risen!"

Joanna would have run to tell the disciples of the incredible discovery. Though they discounted the story as the ravings of hysterical women, Joanna would hardly have doubted herself. For she was a woman who lived in an atmosphere of power. And she had just witnessed a far greater power than Herod's. It was the same power that had healed her.

A woman of high rank, Joanna became part of the intimate circle of Christ's followers, casting her lot with fisherman and poor people rather than the rich and the powerful. God honored her by making her one of the first witnesses of the resurrection.

# The Promise of Joy

Joy comes in the morning. Joanna discovered this in a miraculous way on Jesus' resurrection day. She went to his tomb expecting to minister to his dead body and to grieve. Instead, her sorrow turned to joy. Our joy may not come this morning or tomorrow morning or even the morning after that. We face too many hardships, too many difficult situations, too much sorrow here on earth to think joy will arrive with each morning. But it will come. He's promised. At the end of the day, at the end of this life, there will be a joyful morning for all who trust in him.

*Weeping may remain for a night,*
*but rejoicing comes in the morning.*

PSALM 30:5


*The gift of God is eternal life in Christ*
*Jesus our Lord.*

ROMANS 6:23


*The ransomed of the LORD will return.*
*They will enter Zion with singing;*
*everlasting joy will crown their heads.*
*Gladness and joy will overtake them,*
*and sorrow and sighing will flee away.*

ISAIAH 35:10

Martha

Martha

Martha

Martha

*Which is the*

*feminine form*

*of "lord" and*

*means "lady."*

As Jesus and his disciples were on their way, he came to a village where a woman named Martha opened her home to him. She had a sister called Mary, who sat at the Lord's feet listening to what he said. But Martha was distracted by all the preparations that had to be made. She came to him and asked, "Lord, don't you care that my sister has left me to do the work by myself? Tell her to help me!"

"Martha, Martha," the Lord answered, "you are worried and upset about many things, but only one thing is needed. Mary has chosen what is better, and it will not be taken away from her."

LUKE 10:38–42

## Her Character

Active and pragmatic, she seemed never at a loss for words. Though Jesus chastened her for allowing herself to become worried and upset by small things, she remained his close friend and follower.

---

## Her Sorrow

To have missed an opportunity to simply be with Jesus, loving him and learning from him.

---

## Her Joy

To have Jesus as her friend.

During one of Jesus' frequent stays in their home, Martha became annoyed with Mary. Instead of helping with the considerable chore of feeding and housing Jesus and his disciples, Mary had been sitting at Jesus' feet. Feeling ignored and under-appreciated, Martha marched over to Jesus and demanded: "Lord, don't you care that my sister has left me to do all the work? Tell her to help me."

But Jesus chided her, "Martha, Martha, you are worried about many things, but only one thing is needed. Mary has chosen what is better, and it will not be taken away from her."

Jesus' tender rebuke was carefully calculated to break the grip of Martha's self-pity in order to reveal what was really taking place. Distracted by the need to serve Jesus, she had not taken time to enjoy him, to listen and learn from him.

Martha's story points to what is most important in our lives She seemed confused and distracted, conned into believing her ceaseless activity would produce something of lasting importance. But Martha does more than simply instruct us through her mistakes. She shows what it is like to have a relationship with Jesus so solid that no posturing or hiding is ever necessary. Martha seemed free to be herself in his presence. Where else should she have taken her frustration and anger, after all, but to Jesus?

The more we delve into Martha's story, the more familiar it seems—as familiar as the face gazing at us in the mirror. A woman who placed too much importance on her own activity and not enough on sitting quietly before Jesus, Martha also loved Jesus and was confident of his love for her. As such, she offers a warmly human portrait of what it means to have Jesus as a friend, allowing him to stretch her faith, rebuke her small vision of the world, and show her what the power of God could do.

# The Blessing of Honesty Before God

Bold Martha stands before the Savior of the world and gripes and complains. More than an indictment of her impudent behavior, Martha's story is a portrait of total honesty before God—the beauty of a soul bared. And why not? God surely knows what is within us anyway. And he still loves us. What a blessing honesty before God can be. What a relief to let ourselves be totally known and to be assured that we are still loved—loved enough not to ignore our sin and our bad behavior but to rescue us from it.

*Nothing in all creation is hidden from God's sight. Everything is uncovered and laid bare before the eyes of him to whom we must give account. . . . For we do not have a high priest who is unable to sympathize with our weaknesses, but we have one who has been tempted in every way, just as we are—yet was without sin. Let us then approach the throne of grace with confidence, so that we may receive mercy and find grace to help us in our time of need.*

HEBREWS 4:13, 15–16

*An honest answer
    is like a kiss on the lips.*

PROVERBS 24:26

*I know, my God, that you test the heart and are pleased with integrity.*

1 CHRONICLES 29:17

# Widow with the Two Coins

Widow with the
Two Coins

Widow with the
Two Coins

Widow with the
Two Coins

*Though poor,*

*she gave*

*generously.*

*Jesus sat down opposite the place where the offerings were put and watched the crowd putting their money into the temple treasury. Many rich people threw in large amounts. But a poor widow came and put in two very small copper coins, worth only a fraction of a penny.*

*Calling his disciples to him, Jesus said, "I tell you the truth, this poor widow has put more into the treasury than all the others. They all gave out of their wealth; but she, out of her poverty, put in everything— all she had to live on."*

MARK 12:41–44

## Her Character

Though extremely poor, she is one of the most greathearted people in the Bible. Right after warning his disciples to watch out for the teachers of the law who devour widows' houses, Jesus caught sight of her in the temple. He may have called attention to her as a case in point.

---

## Her Sorrow

To be alone, without a husband to provide for her.

---

## Her Joy

To surrender herself to God completely, trusting him to act on her behalf.

With Passover approaching, the temple was packed with worshipers from all over Israel. Jesus was speaking to his disciples: "Beware of the scribes! They devour widows' houses and for the sake of appearance say long prayers. They will receive the greater condemnation."

Then he sat down opposite the temple treasury, in the court of the women. The place was crowded with people dropping their offerings into one of the thirteen trumpet-shaped receptacles that hung on the walls. Jesus watched as a widow deposited two small copper coins, less than a day's wages.

Jesus continued, "Amen, I say to you, this poor widow put in more than all the other contributors to the treasury. For they have all contributed from their surplus wealth, but she, from her poverty, has contributed all she had, her whole livelihood."

Here was one of the widows he had just spoken of, pressured, perhaps, by unscrupulous men to give beyond her means. Her faith was such a contrast to their greed.

But there is yet another aspect to her story. How easy it would have been for her to conclude that her gift was simply too meager to offer. What need had God for two copper coins? Surely they meant more to her than him. But she gave them anyway. And we are astonished by her generosity.

But what use could God make of such a sacrifice? Maybe, in a manner of speaking, God did need what she had to offer. Perhaps her gesture consoled Jesus a short time before his passion and death. She had given all she had to live on; soon, he would give his life. A widow's copper coins, a man's life— everything offered for the sake of the kingdom.

# The Promise of Provision

God's promise of provision is beautifully illustrated in this story of the widow who gave all she had. She had no one else to rely on, only God. That's true of us as well, isn't it? Regardless of our financial situation, whether financially well-off or constantly skimming the bottom, we have no one else to rely on. Our true security is not in our belongings or our bank accounts, but in God alone. And he has promised to provide.

*Some trust in chariots and some in horses, but we trust in the name of the LORD our God.*

PSALM 20:7

*Jesus said, "Do not worry about your life, what you will eat or drink; or about your body, what you will wear. Is not life more important than food, and the body more important than clothes? Look at the birds of the air; they do not sow or reap or store away in barns, and yet your heavenly Father feeds them. Are you not much more valuable than they?"*

MATTHEW 6:25–26

 is co-author with Carol Cymbala of *He's Been Faithful*. The author of the best-selling books *An Angel a Day* and *A Miracle a Day*, she lives with her two daughters in Belmont, Michigan.

*Jean E. Sysuerda* is a former editor and associate publisher for Zondervan Bibles. While at Zondervan, she was responsible for such best-selling Bibles as the *NIV Women's Devotional Bible,* the *NIV Adventure Bible,* and the *NIV Teen Study Bible.* She is the general editor for the recently released *NIV Women of Faith Study Bible.* She and her husband have three grown children and live in Allendale, Michigan.

*Blessings and Promises Through the Eyes of Women of the Bible* is based on the best-selling book, *Women of the Bible* by Ann Spangler and Jean E. Syswerda. *Women of the Bible* focuses on the lives of 52 remarkable women in Scripture—women whose struggles to live with faith and courage are not unlike our own. This year-long devotional book offers a unique method to help you slow down and savor the story of God's unrelenting love for his people, offering a fresh perspective that will nourish and strengthen your relationship with him.

*Women of the Bible*
*is available at stores everywhere*
*for $16.99 (hardcover).*